Dick

Congratulations
on your Confirmation
the Buermanns

This Game Called Life

THIS GAME CALLED LIFE

Words of Courage
And Inspiration
From the World of Sports

Edited by Rob Wood
Illustrated by David R. Miles

♛ HALLMARK EDITIONS

*For when the One Great Scorer comes
to write against your name,
He marks — not that you won or lost —
but how you played the game.*

GRANTLAND RICE

Peter Dixon is a surfer. When you ask him why he does it, why a man pits his strength and skill against the relentless force of a ten-foot wall of water, he gives you a dozen different reasons. But ultimately, he says, it's the challenge of...

FACING THE SEA AND THE WAVES

There is really no one way to express the feeling that a good ride on a big fast-moving wave brings to surfers. Some surfers get *stoked,* others are exhilarated, a few are blasted, but most feel deeply satisfied when the wave was perfect and the ride long. The experience of surfing has drawn thousands to the waves. New surfers are beginning a sport that started many hundreds of years ago in Polynesia, and after a period of quiet has been born again....

Why the sudden explosive interest in surfing? What draws people into the cold water, to the pounding waves, to the hazards of cuts on sharp coral and collisions with other surfers? Why do surfers fly and drive and sail thousands of miles to be blasted off their board by a wave? Why have thousands and thousands all over the world bought or built boards? And finally what is there about surfing that captures the imagination and satisfies some fulfillment of the mind and body?

There are several qualities to surfing that may provide some answers. Surfing is the most individualistic of all sports. Alone on a board, speeding over a wave at fifteen or twenty miles an hour, the surfer experiences an ecstatic communication with natural forces, a delicious isolation, and total freedom from the anxieties and mundane cares of the workaday world.

Surfing is also a challenge requiring intense concentration. The total range of senses is engaged in keeping the body in balance and the wave from dominating the rider. This is particularly true in big surf. On smaller, well-formed waves there is time to look around, wave to a friend and plan ahead. But the surfer who lets his attention lag will lose to the wave. Waves are living, moving things and, like people, no two waves are alike. This infinite variety gives surfing color, excitement, action. Yet surfing is uncomplicated. In the frightfully complex world of modern technology nothing is quite as refreshingly simple as a functional surfboard and waves, sun, and sky.

Surfers as a rule are not worriers. I've never experienced a worry sitting on a board waiting for a wave and I've never known a surfer who was troubled out on the water. This escape from the ordinary is certainly a part of surfing, as is the feeling of being unique. Many have observed that younger surfers start the sport because of the status it gives them. But whatever the motivation, the surfer must still face the sea and the waves.

James Ramsey Ullman, journalist and
member of the successful American Mount
Everest Expedition of 1963, writes about the
challenge he knows so well...

BECAUSE IT'S THERE!

Challenge is the core and mainspring of all human activity. If there's an ocean, we cross it; if there's a disease, we cure it; if there's a wrong, we right it; if there's a record, we break it; and finally, if there's a mountain, we climb it.

Wimbledon champion Althea Gibson is
often called "the Jackie Robinson of tennis."
She's an expert at coming up the hard way.
Early in life on the streets of Harlem, she
learned how to look out for herself. She
learned how to be…

TOUGH ENOUGH TO TAKE IT

I always wanted to be somebody. I guess that's why I kept running away from home when I was a kid even though I took some terrible whippings for it. It's why I took to tennis right away and kept working at it, even though I was the wildest tomboy you ever saw and my strong likings were a mile away from what the tennis people wanted me to do. It's why I've been willing to live like a gypsy all these years….

…Having to contend with crowds hostile to me because of my color, with newspapermen demanding twice as much of me as they did of anybody else simply because my color made me more newsworthy, and even with powerful governments seeking to use me as an instrument of national policy because of my color, seemed to me to be more than anybody should have to bear….

If I've made it, it's half because I was game to take a wicked amount of punishment along the way and half because there were an awful lot of people who cared enough to help me. It has been a bewildering, challenging, exhausting experience, often more pain-ful than pleasurable, more sad than happy. But I wouldn't have missed it for the world.

Jim Ryun broke the world record for the mile with a time of 3:51.1. But the road to success is not easy. He was successful in the 1964 Olympic trials because he forced himself to...

TRY HARDER

"It was a breakthrough race," he says. They ran it at the Los Angeles Coliseum, in September of 1964, and seven men lined up to see which three would line up again half a world away. "I was in last place with 150 yards to go," Ryun recalls. "I thought, 'I've put in an awful lot of work to finish this way.' So I told myself, 'Try harder.'"

Ahead of him were six men, but only three counted, the first three, Burleson, O'Hara and Grelle. Ryun drove up to Grelle's shoulder, and then with the tape just ahead, he summoned whatever it is men sum-mon. He edged out Grelle at the tape, and made the trip to Tokyo....

...In the States, other milers have learned to handle the boxes, the shoving crowd. Burleson and Beatty shouted men out of the way, announced they were coming through, and then made their move. With others, you got out of the way, or you got trampled.

Not Ryun. He disdains such methods. "I have never told a man in front of me to move over because I was coming through. It is his race, too, and he has the right to be there. If I get into a box, I have to get out. I have to run outside. I never will burst through." He repeats it all; it is a way of life…."If the fellow's there, why not go around him? You got yourself there; it's your obligation to get yourself out."

But beyond the unwillingness to shout or shove a man out of the way, there is more. Jim Ryun subscribes to the philosophy of pain. He does not control other men in the race, but he controls himself. Look at the pictures of Ryun winning the big races, his body erect as a Marine's, his eyes clear and intent, his jaw set. He may be a boy, but he looks like a man then. A 10th of a second past the tape, and the pain becomes visible. His eyes roll back in their sockets, his head lolls on a broken swan's neck, the mouth opens wide for precious oxygen, the arms flap like a doll's. He gives in, finally, to the luxury of exhaustion.

But he has won….

ARNOLD HANO

11

*Golf great Ben Hogan worked to get where
he is today. He has survived a near-fatal car
crash. He has battled old age and hardship.
Yet he keeps on working because...*

THAT FELLA'S NEVER SATISFIED

The day after the Colonial Tournament, in which he
played respectably at the age of 57, Ben Hogan...said,
"A fella's never satisfied, I guess." His voice halted
meaningfully. "But..."

...The year 1970 was made when William Benjamin
Hogan, his swollen left knee squeezed into an elastic
brace, limped intently out of retirement to finish ninth
in the Houston Champions International and challenge briefly in the Colonial, which he has won five
times.

Imagine Joe DiMaggio donning his old uniform and
coming off the bench to rip a grand-slam home run
before a capacity crowd in Yankee Stadium, and you
have some idea of the drama that drenched Hogan's
performances on two of the most arduous courses
in the sport.

The short return to professional golf of the man
widely considered the greatest player ever, a winner
of all four major championships, a national hero after
he overcame the near-fatal effects of a 1949 car-bus
crash, gives rise to fascinating questions. Why did he
do it? What is his life like today?...

Early every afternoon, his leg and the weather per-
mitting, he will empty an old shag bag and hit balls
for 40 to 90 minutes, starting with a nine-iron and
working through the set. With each club he will hit
basic shots, then, before putting it away, will hit two
different types of shots, moving the ball to the right
or left, or hitting it low or high. "The basics of the
swing remain the same," he says. "But I'm always experimenting, looking for better ways to hit finesse
shots. I never hit a shot on the course I haven't prac-
ticed." His clear voice, neutral at first, takes on more
of the drawling intonations of Texas as he warms to
talking. "I'm a curious person. Experimenting is my
enjoyment....

...."There is so much more of everything today. More
players, more tournaments. There are more good
players, of course, and the best ones might be better.
Competition improves people. Fifteen years from now
the level of play will be better still. You have to beat
the competition. To do that you have to find a way.
You have to have an edge." Hogan's voice hardens, as
if he were himself hungering for that edge all over
again. "The fundamentals of swinging are the same,
but the technique of hitting the ball has improved,
and the equipment is slightly better...not as much
better as the individual and his technique. All golf
shots are missed to a degree. Today fewer are missed.
These boys think better. They're bigger and stronger,

14

and they practice harder. These fellas putt better —
more boldly. That's due to practice. When I started,
they used to laugh at me for practicing.

"The fella who starts today has a better chance to
be a real good player than I did. The facts are all laid
out for him. All you have to do is read and apply what
you read through hard work. I had to dig it out for
myself. It took me from age 12 to age 35, trying things,
proving and disproving." Hogan paused and studied
his clasped, permanently calloused hands, then said,
"But maybe that made me a better player, a better
competitor. Most of the enjoyment in life is in improv-
ing. If I didn't think I could improve right now, why…"
He shook his head sideways and stopped, appalled.

NICK SEITZ

UPS AND DOWNS OF LIFE

I just guess the sun don't shine on the same dawg's
tail every day.

SAMUEL JACKSON SNEAD
after a play-off victory over Ben Hogan

Betty Meade, national squash rackets
champion, had won it all. Now after a tragic,
crippling accident she has it all to do over.
But the future is always the real test of a champion.
What does it take to pick up the pieces and
begin again? It takes faith, determination, and
something very special. Some call it...

COURAGE!

Betty Meade is beautiful.

They went years without letting a woman attend the Philadelphia Sports Writers Banquet and then they invited Betty Meade, who is beautiful. For years, men have been standing up at these banquets mumbling platitudes about why people play games.

Then they invited Betty Meade, who is beautiful. She stood there with her blonde hair glinting like a halo in the spotlight. She came out there in her gray dress with the fur trim, and her net stockings, and the artificial leg in the right stocking, and she told it better than it had ever been told before.

"Competing in athletics helps you to face problems," she said, and guys who had been babbling drunkenly all evening were struck silent. "In sports, you have to fight for everything you get. Nobody is going to hand you anything.

"You learn to lose. The first five or six years I played tennis I did a lot more losing than winning.

16

Athletic competition helps you to learn to face anything in life. When I lost my leg, it was another loss. I'd have to face life, to learn to walk again, to run again."

At banquets, everybody always talks about winning. Then they invited Betty Meade and she gave them a lesson in humility and faith and courage. That's why they invited her, to honor her as the year's Most Courageous Athlete.

She won the national squash singles last year. And the doubles. And the mixed doubles. And two days after she won the singles, her legs were smashed in an auto accident. They were able to mend the left leg, which was broken in two places. They had to amputate the right leg below the knee.

"I was near hysterics," her husband Newton Meade remembered. "She looked up at me and said, 'Don't worry about me, I'll be okay. Take care of yourself.' I knew damn well she wasn't going to be okay. But that shows her attitude, right there."...

Betty Meade's father was a minister. "You believe when you're growing up," she said quietly. "And you go off to college and maybe you begin to doubt it. Then you find something to believe in again.

"The thing that was such tremendous strength to me was that so many people were praying for me. That's the main reason I wasn't depressed, why I didn't go into a tailspin.

"People who had never prayed before prayed for me.

17

A man who always said he was an agnostic wrote me that he got down on his knees. When I read that I thought that maybe this accident was for the best.

"I had played so much and accomplished so much. I was older. Maybe it was easier for me to adjust. When you play sports you learn to win and to lose. You become accustomed to losing without taking it home with you and making everyone miserable. When it's over, it's over.

"Athletes seem to have a much healthier attitude. There's a difference between a good loser and learning how to lose. I was never a good loser, but losing teaches you something."

She is back playing squash. She has played eight rounds of golf including a round of 102. Her husband bet her $100 she wouldn't break 100 before the year ended, but he knows he does not have to invent challenges.

"She's working with weights to strengthen her upper leg," he said, beaming at her. "And she'll start on sprints soon, six or seven steps at a time. Before, her shot-making and determination made the difference. She can still beat 50 percent of the squash players in her present condition. Nothing she does will surprise me. I'm just proud to be part of her."

She stood there last night, her serenity flooding the big room like some kind of torch. The poker players in the raucous crowd recognized that she was willing to play the cruel hand she was dealt. There was faith and humility and courage for even the fuzziest eyes to see. Betty Meade, you're beautiful.

STAN HOCHMAN

John C. Tobin, championship skier, has raced the powder trails all over snow country. There is nothing, he says, like...

THE SWEET CUP OF VICTORY

The racer's entire drive is focused on preparing himself for proficiency in the art of racing. As much as he loves to ski and to be in the ski country, the real sweetness of life is victory. The sense of attainment is unbelievably high for the racer who has faced up to his fears, worked out a plan of attack, and then put together a medal-winning performance.

*Floyd Patterson fought back against long
odds to rewrite boxing lore as the only man
ever to regain the world heavyweight
championship. The black man from Dixie returned
the title to the United States by stopping
Sweden's Ingemar Johansson with a thunderous
left hook. Patterson always was a hard and
punishing fighter. Yet here he reveals
a remarkable sensitivity, as he tells...*

WHAT I HAVE LEARNED

...As a child I was never at ease at home or in school or in the streets. I was embarrassed most of the time, shamed at other times, smothered in a feeling of inadequacy. In school I was too frightened to speak. I had a fear of being inferior. When I first started to court my wife, I'd look at her and say nothing. I had few friends, no interests, nothing of which I could be proud, no clothes, no real talent except for making myself miserable. I was one of "The Lost Ones," which was the way they described me when I was first sent to Wiltwyck School, a farm for emotionally disturbed youngsters, at Esopus, New York, back in September, 1945, when I was ten....

I'm a grown man now...and I've learned finally that the world is a place in which to live, not a cellar in which you hide. There was a time when you could hit me and I wouldn't think much of it, but you could

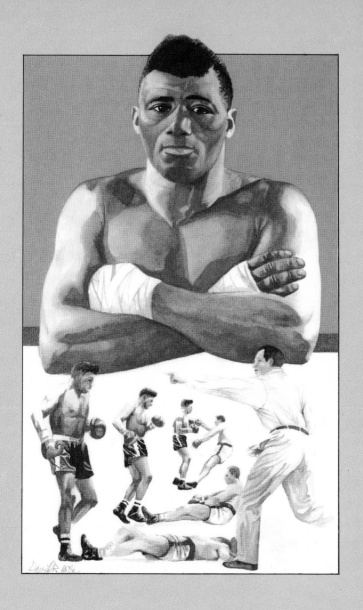

say something and it would hurt me terribly. In that respect, at least, I haven't changed much, although I know now that what is said depends upon who the person is that's saying it.

Now I'm saying it and I find it isn't easy. I have something special to say, but I don't think I'm somebody special....

...I have no intention of preaching a sermon this late in the story of my life, but it does seem to me that all people should be treated alike until you discover for yourself that one is better or more likeable or more honest or more decent than the other.

For myself, I approach everybody in one way. They all are 100 per cent, and I let them find their own level. Some go up to 110 per cent or more. Some drop down so much that before we're through they owe me some points. You can't like everybody, but you can't dislike everybody, either. And so far as hate goes, there aren't too many people in the whole world who are so bad that you must hate them.

There must be room in all of us for understanding. Coming from a fighter that may seem a strange thought to some people. Ours is the only business in which the fundamental idea is to knock the other guy unconscious, and if you follow that thought through to its logical conclusion, it is the only sport in which a man has a license to hurt another man.

Yet there isn't hate in any one of us.

Race driver Allen Heath lost a hand and almost his life in a spectacular track accident. He came back to win again as the "One-Armed Bandit" of racing. He could have quit. He could have felt sorry for himself. But Heath tells it like it is...

YOU CAN'T EAT SYMPATHY

...Hell, I haven't done anything anyone else couldn't do if they wanted to do it badly enough. Being a race driver is tough. Being a race driver with a hook for a hand is a lot tougher. But if it couldn't have been done, I couldn't have done it. I'm not made of iron. People think I'm not for real. Hell, I bruise as much as the next guy. What hurts them hurts me. It's just that hurtin' never bothered me as much and sure never stopped me from doin' what I wanted to do.

When you get hurt like I did, if you want to lay down and cry, you can. I didn't want to. I didn't want to feel sorry for myself and give up. I had a boxful of sympathy cards, but you can't eat that sympathy. I realized I had to accept what had happened and make the best of it.

23

*Coach Vince Lombardi knew victory as few
men do. He preached dedication. He preached
hard work and sacrifice. And every year Coach
Lombardi told his squad that...*

PRIDE WINS!

"I've never been with a loser, gentlemen, and I don't
intend to start at this late date. You're here to play
football, and I'm here to see you play as well as your
God-given abilities will allow. And that means total
dedication. I want total dedication from every man in
this room, dedication to himself, to the team, and to
winning. Winning is a habit, gentlemen. Winning
isn't everything, it's the only thing. If you can shrug
off a loss, you can't be a winner. The harder you work,
the harder it is to lose. And I'm going to see that you
work, I'm going to push you and push you and push
you because I get paid to win and so do you. Football
is a violent game. To play you have to be tough. Phys-
ically tough and mentally tough. And you've got to
have pride, because when two teams meet that are
equal in ability and execution, it's the team that has
pride that wins. Gentlemen, let's be winners! There's
nothing like it."

Olympic champion Bob Richards is both a minister and an athlete. Candid and plain-spoken, he gives new meaning to the old adage "Winners never quit and quitters never win," when he talks about...

A QUALITY OF SOUL

...I have never really seen a great champion who quit when he was beaten: he somehow has that quality of soul that refuses to go down; he bounces back to an even greater victory. In 1948 we were in the Dyche Stadium in Chicago for the Olympic trials. There was a boy there who was acclaimed as probably the finest Olympic prospect America had, a fellow by the name of Harrison Dillard....I happen to know Harrison personally. We have made a number of trips together, and have roomed together. I think he is one of the greatest athletes I have ever met. I saw Harrison as he got down to his mark in the 110-meter hurdles. He hadn't been beaten in eighty-three consecutive races. In two and a half years no one had come close to him. He was the prime hurdler of the world. They got down to their marks — six boys; of those six, only three could qualify for the Olympic team. They were out there giving everything they had. They got set. The gun went off. Harrison lunged out to an early lead. He was about a yard and a half ahead at the first hurdle. But somehow he overstrode and hit the second hurdle. He practically fell down on the third and stumbled and draped himself over the last hurdle.

I'll never forget it as long as I live. I was standing nearby and I saw Harry come up off that hurdle and look down the track. His lower jaw dropped and that cold realization of defeat began to creep into his face and I wondered if a fellow could ever feel worse. He had missed the Olympic teams, and an Olympic championship that was a cinch was gone because he couldn't even represent the United States. Could a fellow *ever* feel worse?

Harrison told me afterwards that right there, at that hurdle, looking down the track and watching those boys go on to claim his berth on the team, he made one of the greatest decisions of his running career. That was to come back and to change defeat into victory. And so, a few moments later, he qualified for the 100-meters. He barely made the team for third place by nosing out Eddie Conwell *by a quarter of an inch.*

They went to London. No one gave this made-over hurdler a chance. But when they got down on their marks in Wembley Stadium, one of them was a fellow who knew how to take defeat. When the gun went off before 100,000 people, he lunged out, dug in with everything he had, hit the tape in 10.3 to tie Jesse Owens' Olympic record. He had won the 100-meter championship, an event not his own, to claim probably the greatest championship of his life.

27

Four years later in Helsinki I saw him run his specialty, the hurdles, in 13.7 to win another Olympic championship. It's that sort of thing that makes a champion. They don't quit when they're beaten. They bounce back to an even more glorious victory. They not only do it in competition; they do it in life.

Gale Sayers, premier running back of the Chicago Bears, suffered a crippling knee injury in 1968. Fans feared that this was the end of the line for one of the greatest grid stars of the mid sixties. But Sayers came back. He came back big. He came back because he called on...

FACTOR X

"Sayers will fold up like an accordion when he gets hit."

That was one question Sayers hoped to settle right away in the game with the Redskins. But he was disappointed to learn, earlier in the week, that he would not start, that he would be used only to run back kickoffs and punts....

All along, Sayers had refused to baby himself....
Right after the cast was removed, he began to lift weights on the leg. He started jogging in early February. He was examined on February 27, and Dr. Theodore Fox, who had performed the operation, told

Sayers, "If there were a game this Sunday, you'd be able to play."

Dr. Fox believes in Sayers. He once defined the special quality that made Sayers the finest runner in football. "Factor X," he called it. "This stands for drive and motivation," he said. "Factor X elevates a player one plateau. It makes a star out of an average player and a superstar out of a star." Dr. Fox said that his operation on Sayers' knee would contribute 60 percent to Sayers' recovery and "Gale's strong desire to return — Factor X — will add the other 40 percent."

There could be no doubt about that desire. "I worked hard to get up there," Sayers had said midpoint in his recuperation period, "and I'm going to work twice as hard to stay up there." At that time, an article in a Chicago newspaper suggested that running backs with knee injuries rarely come back to top form and that Sayers might have to spend the rest of his career as a flanker or at some other position. The article infuriated Gale. "I saved it," he said, "because when I do come back as a runner, I'm gonna show it to him." And then, as if to underscore his determination, he drew out the words — "I...Will...Be...Back."...

Now it was 7:30....The Bears were the receiving team. Gale Sayers was deep, at his five-yard line, with Ross Montgomery stationed just in front of him. Just as the kicker moved forward, Sayers hollered to Montgomery to deploy right. Sayers, who captains the kick and punt return team, always tells the other deep back where to go. The idea is for Sayers to cover three-quarters of the field, to make sure that he gets the football.

He got the football. He took it easily on his six-yard line and started straight up the middle. One man broke through the wedge and came on to challenge Sayers. "I feel I can always beat any man one-on-one," Sayers has said, "and two-on-one I can beat 75 percent of the time." Sayers gave the one man his inside move, a head and shoulder fake, and the man was out of it and Sayers was flashing to the right, toward the sidelines....

Sayers was in full stride now, streaking down the sidelines. Two Washington defensive backs angled in on him around the Redskin 40. One lunged at him and Sayers just pushed him away with his left arm. The other threw himself at Sayers, jostling him momentarily. But Sayers kept his feet, regained control and sped triumphantly into the end zone. There was a purity, a shining purity to that run....The first time he had carried the ball in combat since his knee injury, which was the worst kind of a knee injury you can have, he had broken one. It was as if all the questions had been answered, all the doubts resolved about the condition of Gale Sayers....

AL SILVERMAN

31

"Man can go as far and as fast as he wants,"
claims Roger Bannister. He proved that on a
cold, clammy English Thursday in 1954 by
breaking the four-minute mile...

BREAKING
THE PSYCHOLOGICAL BARRIER

Chataway led but all eyes were on Bannister. He was the important figure. The race was almost half over and he hardly seemed to be in it at all. That was his method. Hang back. Stay away. Save, conserve, rest. Be ready for the finish.

"The time for the half mile, 1 minute and 58.2 seconds," shouted the announcer....

"If the pace were not fast enough," explained Bannister, "I would have taken over the lead at the half."

No need. Bannister stayed in second place. Chataway was running the greatest race of his life. He was pouring every ounce of energy into the third quarter. He did not care. He was part of history. Onward....

Now it was the south straightaway again. Chataway still in the lead. By 3 yards. Then 2. Then shoulder to shoulder. At the bottom of the south end of the track, Roger Bannister took over the lead.

"The time for three quarters," said the announcer, over the growing screams of the crowd, "3 minutes and .5 seconds."

It could be done. Now it was possible. Bannister had

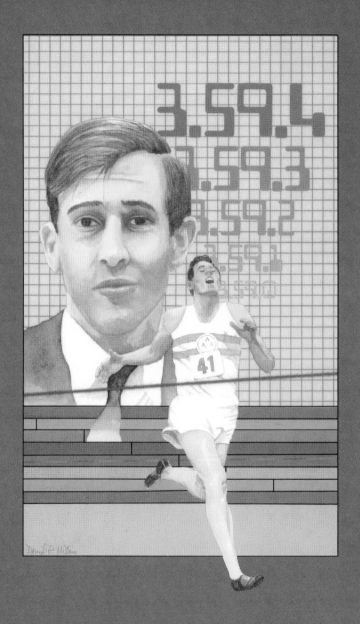

run three quarters of a mile in slightly over 3 minutes. If he could run the last quarter of a mile in under 1 minute he would do it. The problem was stamina.

"When I heard the three-quarter time I began to move out just as fast and hard as I could. I was where I had planned. My body felt ready," he said.

Up the north end of the track he turned, harder, harder, harder. The crowd standing, their voices, their arms, their hearts pushing Bannister toward the end of the race....

Down to the finish line. His legs burned, his eyes smarted from the wind, his heart beating rapidly but his mind was serenely blank.

"There is no time to think at that stage, no time to decide what to do or what you have done," he said. "There is just a trained body acting in a trained way."

Now the last, lunging, final stride, his chest cracking against the tape, his body quivering, his arms pushing across the line. It was over. He had reached the end.

The small fingers had stopped the four watches timing the meet. The judges came together on the track to examine their times. This was the important decision.

They nodded in agreement, they shook their watches and waved to the stands. They were filled with joy. They, too, had played a part in history. The time was relayed to the announcer.

He gathered his strength and announced to the

crowd, "The time for Roger Bannister, 3 minutes…"

He could not be heard after that. He had said the magic words. The official time for the mile was 3 minutes and 59.4 seconds….

The psychological barrier was broken. Man was no longer incapable of running a mile in under 4 minutes….

In 1967 Jim Ryun, a student at the University of Kansas, ran a mile in 3 minutes and 51.1 seconds for the world record….

"There is no limit," Dr. Roger Bannister was to say years after cracking the 4-minute mark. "Man can go as fast and as far as he wants."

MAURY ALLEN

Bobby Jones, world's only winner of the Grand Slam of Golf, knows the difference between…

GOOD...BETTER...BEST!

The difference between the good and great golfers is in their putting. The good golfers are happy to sink a difficult putt. The great golfers know they must sink a difficult putt.

It was mid season and Coach Knute Rockne was
hospitalized with phlebitis and a dangerous
blood clot in his leg. Notre Dame was slated to
play rival Carnegie Tech. Rockne left his bed
to coach the game. Rockne risked his life that
day because he wanted...

VICTORY MORE THAN LIFE

The door opened. Tom Lieb came in, carrying Rockne in his arms, as if he were a baby. Lieb placed Rockne on a table. He sat there, legs stretched out, staring ahead....His face was very sober, very set. His eyes were static. This was like watching a calm over mercury.

For five minutes he sat there, immobile. The seconds were long in a football locker room where boys were dressed, waiting to run and explode. Time was running out. Two o'clock would be soon. But Rock looked at nobody, seemed hardly conscious of anybody or anything about him.

The boys were sitting before him, on benches, like they do in a grade-school picture. They were like grade-school kids as they looked at him, away from him, bit their lips, glanced at the floor, did other things to get through that silence — the boys who were to make football history by winning nineteen straight tough games and two successive national championships....

It would have been ludicrous if it had not been serious — the great, strong, fierce, indomitable, dynamic Rockne being carried into a locker room like a baby....

There were about five of us back of the lockers where we could see but not be seen. There were some wet eyes. You may think this a very silly business to get so emotional about, but this was in 1929, just a few days before the stock market crashed and a new era dawned. This was Rockne and Notre Dame; and across the way were Steffen and Carnegie Tech, the tormentors.

Behind the lockers Dr. Maurice Keady was whispering: "If he lets go, and that clot dislodges, hits his heart or his brain — he's got an even chance of never leaving this dressing room alive."

It began. When his voice came it was strong. This is close to an actual record of the words he used:

"A lot of water has gone under the bridge since I first came to Notre Dame — but I don't know when I've ever wanted to win a game as badly as this one.

"I don't care what happens after today.

"Why do you think I'm taking a chance like this? To see you lose?" (He was beginning to shout.)

"They'll be primed. They'll be tough. They think they have your number. *Are you going to let it happen again?*"

Quiet again. I don't know what the boys were doing.

I could not see. All of us behind the lockers had heads down.

Now he shot the works. He let go. I watched his face through a space between the lockers. As he talked his mobile features distorted with almost insane determination. This was the supreme effort of a great fighter. His voice was vibrant, strong:

"Go out there and crack 'em. Crack 'em. *Crack 'em.* Fight to live. Fight to win. Fight to live. *Fight to win — win — win —* WIN —"...

They were leaving, running, leaving a savage roar among the reverberating tiles. As the last of them left, Rock collapsed.

His eyes were shut. His face was in pain. He was sweating. The doctor, at his side throughout, felt the pulse, gently mopped the sweat from his face.

Rock wanted to win more than he wanted to live.

FINAL SCORE: Notre Dame-7 / Carnegie Tech-0

FRANCIS WALLACE

Mental attitude is the crucial difference
between a good pitcher and some cherry
chucker in the minor leagues. So says
Johnny Sain, pitching coach, and former
ace of the Boston Braves.

THE POWER OF POSITIVE PITCHING

The woods are full of pitchers going back to the minor leagues and bullpens who throw just as good a fast ball and curve as the guys who're winning in the big leagues. Why? They've all got a thousand reasons why the sun's liable not to come up tomorrow. Well, the world wants winners and results. People don't want to hear about labor pains. They want to see the baby.

...Look, you can go stomping through weeds and popping birds out of the sky if you're a good shot and shoot subconsciously. But if you stand there all nerved up like you are in a ball game and say, "Step number one, put finger on trigger; step number two, do this" — well, you couldn't hit a sleeping elephant. It's the same in pitching. And the only reason a good arm can't pitch in the big leagues is not thinking you can do it. But praying isn't gonna get that ball across the plate. You've got to *know* it's gonna go there and have a program to get it there!

How many of us live life to the fullest?
Francis Chichester did. He circled the world,
alone in a 53-foot boat. Why did he accept
the challenge? Because he believed...

IT'S THE EFFORT THAT COUNTS

When he was 52, Chichester decided to set forth on the greatest adventure of his life. His boat, the Gipsy Moth IV, a sea-going ketch, 53 feet in length, was normally manned by a crew of six. On August 27, 1966, Francis Chichester sailed off in the Gipsy Moth IV from Plymouth, England, as the lone passenger and the lone crewman. Objective: to sail around the world.

"The only way to live in the full," said the dauntless Englishman, "is doing something which depends on physical action, on the senses, and at the same time on the man-developed parts of the brain." It was to be a harrowing trip, a challenge if he, one man, could manage a vessel that normally required six stalwarts under racing conditions. When he reached the treacherous waters of Cape Horn, squalls as strong as 100 knots an hour rocked his ketch and frigid waves spilled over his deck. Five times his cockpit was flooded, and Chichester was in mortal peril.

Yet against all odds, the man succeeded and Britain paid him homage. Queen Elizabeth was so impressed with the exploit that she knighted him while he was still at sea. In all, Sir Francis covered 28,500 miles in a voyage that took him 226 days. Safely ashore, Sir Francis once again reiterated his philosophy: "It's the effort that counts, not the success." And the trip must certainly stand as one of the greatest physical efforts ever made by a man past fifty.

JIM BENAGH

Johnny Bench, All Star catcher for the Cincinnati Reds, talks about...

THE COURAGE OF CONVICTION

I know I'm too frank for some people, but there are too many false things in this world and I don't want to be a part of it. If you say what you think, you're called cocky and conceited. But if you have an object in life, you shouldn't be afraid to stand up and say it.

Breaking the color barrier in baseball was a
courageous achievement for the man, Jackie
Robinson, and the man who made it possible —
Branch Rickey. This is the way it was as
the Dodger boss asked Robinson to give his all.
And history shows that...

ROBINSON MEASURED UP

..."Do you know why you were brought here?"

"Not exactly. I heard something about a colored team at Ebbets Field. That it?"

"No...that isn't it." Rickey studied the dark face, the half-open mouth, the widened and worried eyes. Then he said, "You were brought here, Jackie, to play for the Brooklyn organization. Perhaps on Montreal to start with — "

"Me? Play for Montreal?" the player gasped.

Rickey nodded. "If you can make it, yes. Later on — also if you can make it — you'll have a chance with the Brooklyn Dodgers."

Robinson could only nod at this point.

"I want to win pennants and we need ballplayers!" Rickey whacked the desk. He sketched the efforts and the scope of his two-year search for players of promise. "Do *you* think you can do it? Make good in organized baseball?"

Robinson shifted to relieve his mounting tension.

"If...if I got the chance," he stammered.

"There's more here than just *playing,* Jackie," Rickey warned. "I wish it meant only hits, runs and errors — things you can see in a box score…"

"Can you do it? Can you do it?" Rickey asked over and over.

Shifting nervously, Robinson looked from Rickey to Sukeforth as they talked of his arms and legs and swing and courage. Did he have the guts to play the game no matter what happened? Rickey pointed out the enormity of the responsibility for all concerned: owners of the club, Rickey, Robinson and all baseball. The opposition would shout insults, come in spikes first, throw at his head.

"Mr. Rickey," Robinson said, "they've been throwing at my head for a long time."

Rickey's voice rose. "Suppose I'm a player…in the heat of an important ball game." He drew back as if to charge at Robinson. "Suppose I collide with you at second base. When I get up, I yell, 'You dirty, black son of a —'" He finished the castigation and added calmly, "What do you do?"

Robinson blinked. He licked his lips and swallowed.

"Mr. Rickey," he murmured, "do you want a ball-player who's afraid to fight back?"

"I want a ballplayer with guts enough *not* to fight back?" Rickey exclaimed almost savagely. He paced across the floor and returned with finger pointing. "You've got to do this job with base hits and stolen

43

bases and fielding ground balls, Jackie. *Nothing else!*"...

"Now I'm playing against you in a World Series!" Rickey stormed and removed his jacket for greater freedom. Robinson's hands clenched, trembled from the rising tension. "I'm a hotheaded player. I want to win that game, so I go into you spikes first, but you don't give ground. You stand there and jab the ball into my ribs and the umpire yells, 'Out!' I flare up — all I see is your face — that black face right on top of me —"

Rickey's bespectacled face, glistening with sweat, was inches from Robinson's at this point. He yelled into the motionless mask, "So I haul off and punch you right in the cheek!"

An oversized fist swung through the air and barely missed Robinson's face. He blinked, but his head didn't move.

"What do you do?" Rickey roared.

"Mr. Rickey," he whispered, "I've got two cheeks. That it?"...

ARTHUR MANN

On April 10, 1947, Branch Rickey announced:

The Brooklyn Dodgers today purchased the contract of Jackie Roosevelt Robinson from the Montreal Royals. He will report immediately.

In sports, as in life, there are absolutes, and as soccer commentator Danny Blanchflower makes clear in answering his critics...

THERE IS ONLY ONE TRUTH

"We didn't like part of your commentary on Sunday," one of them said.

"What was that?" I asked.

"You criticized the St. Louis goalkeeper. Couldn't you have been more positive?"

"No," I replied. "He made a mistake."

"That's not what we mean....You *could* have said it was a good shot."

"It wasn't a bad shot," I admitted, "but the quality of the shot is relative to the goalkeeper's reaction. It happens quickly, and one's best judgment is instinctive. This shot was from nearly 35 yards out. Only a rare one from that distance should beat the goalkeeper, and then one would say, 'Great Shot! The keeper had no chance.' Here the goalkeeper was a yard or more off his goal line into the field of play, a bad position that allowed the ball to glide over his upstretched hand and dip into the empty goal behind. Had he been on his goal line that would not have happened."

"We think you could have said it was a good shot," they insisted.

"It would not be the truth," I said.

"We don't want you to tell lies," they argued. "We

think there are two truths: a positive truth and a negative truth. We want you to be positive — to say it was a good play rather than bad."

I had never met men before who worshipped two truths. Why had such inventive sorts stopped at only two, I wondered? Why not four truths? Or 10? The philosophical winds of it swept through my mind. If they had two truths they must have two gods.... Honor thy father and thy mother and thy two gods.... Positive and Negative....But if there was no bad, how could there be good?...

"I know only one truth," I eventually said..."to which a man takes either a positive or negative attitude."

THE ESSENTIAL DIFFERENCE

The important thing in the Olympic Games is not to win, but to take part. The essential thing is not to have conquered, but to have fought well.

BARON PIERRE DE COUBERTIN,
who was responsible
for beginning the modern
Olympic Games in 1896

Bart Starr, former quarterback of the Green Bay Packers, tells what makes a winner...

THE 3 D's

Whenever I have the pleasure of talking with young people around the country I spend a while describing what I call the "3 D's."

1) *Dedication* — an enthusiastic willingness to accept, even look forward to, the long hours of practice, conditioning and preparation necessary for excellence in any type of endeavor.

2) *Desire* — Maintaining, within, a constant, everburning fire to excell. With it you have the stamina, both mental and physical, to put in those long hours.

3) *Discipline* — Possessing the inner strength to *commit* yourself to the rules, regulations and training needed to achieve excellence — and sticking to them.

To me, team success comes before personal glory. And so it should with you. Thank God for your talents so that you will be humble in victory and gracious in defeat.

Do these things...and you will not only be a better football player, but a well rounded person who is an asset to your team, your community, your country.

Being blind is not a handicap to athlete Bob Anderson. Instead, he regards it as a challenge and has become…

THE BLIND COACH
WHO LEADS THE WAY

William A. (Bob) Anderson is a remarkable blind athlete whose philosophy is "Blindness isn't a handicap; it's a challenge."…

You'd hardly believe Coach Anderson is totally blind. He's handsome, sixty, grey-haired, with warm brown eyes and a ready laugh. Born in Wyoming, one of fourteen children, he was on a promising boxing career when a "rabbit punch" injured his optic nerve. Eight months later he was blind at age twenty-two.

He knows how easy it is to give up. "For a long while I couldn't talk about it." Eventually, he found work as a nightwatchman, park assistant, and blacksmith's helper.

But he loved sports. He wondered if he could learn to bowl, although blind. He did. The guide rail he developed to pace his steps and show when to release the ball is now used over the country.

At the bowling alley, Bob met the famous Patty Berg, woman golf champion. "Do you think you could teach me to play golf?" "Sure," she answered. With her help he learned to line up a putt by sound. Later he became World Champion Blind Bowler and also

World Champion Blind Golfer....

"It's been my long-time dream to make outdoor sports and competitive athletics available to the blind," says Bob. "These kids need to learn how to judge speed and distance when they're out in traffic. A blind child, too, should have a chance to swing a bat or roller skate."

Sometimes he's had to visit a home to convince parents to let their child participate. "A lot of blind kids were shoved in a corner at home. They didn't play with anyone. Through sports, they became little champions in their homes. There's plenty the blind and handicapped can do."

He's living proof, and the children know it. He's someone to admire, to emulate. Said blind Daron Torrance, "I couldn't believe it when they told me all the things he could do. I thought, 'I hope I can be like that.'"...

Bob Anderson emphasizes what life can *offer*. After thirty years of blindness he says, "There's nothing so rewarding as to make people realize they're worthwhile in this world."

DOROTHY P. BREWSTER

Bob Pettit, a basketball superstar who
became the game's first 20,000-point scorer,
was a true leader on the court. It's the same
in life. Bob Pettit is a leader because he
accepts responsibility. Bob says,
no matter who you are...

SOMEBODY LOOKS TO YOU

...I came to realize there is more to life than just those things which satisfy my own desires. Too many athletes are interested in getting what they can out of a sport. Not enough of them think about what they can contribute to a sport and to their fellow man by good example.

Some years ago, I gave a talk at Lake Geneva, Wisconsin, and met a young man named Bill Bradley who had just graduated from high school and was attending his first FCA conference.

Several years later I was in Estes Park and I ran into Bill Bradley there. Bill was then a senior at Princeton and the greatest college basketball player in the country. He was giving a talk to 700 younger people. During that evening he mentioned my talk of three years ago and how that talk had been a great inspiration in his life.

He said he had been confused, and listening to me helped straighten him out a little and get him back on the proper path. This was the nicest thing that has ever been said to me or about me and it proved to me how you can reach young people.

This responsibility does not belong only to athletes. No matter who you are there is somebody looking to you for leadership and guidance.

Rocky Graziano, former middleweight
champion of the world, says...
DO IT TO WIN

...I love this life and this country and I thank God for everything. Like I always said, Somebody up there must like me, and I will never forget where my good luck come from. If I learned any lesson, it is "Whatever you do, do it hard and do it to win." It worked for me.

Babe Didrikson Zaharias was named
the greatest female athlete of the first
half of this century. She was an Olympic
champion. Although golf was her favorite,
there was no sport she didn't love. She was
a champion because...

SHE LIVED BY THE RULES

There've been times when I've almost wished I didn't know the rules so well. In 1946 I was at Spring Lake, New Jersey, playing in the Spring Lake Women's Open. I started out in the qualifying round and shot the first four holes in one under par. On the fifth hole my tee shot sliced off into the rough. I went over there and played out a nice iron shot to the green.

I finished that hole, and the sixth one. After holing out on the sixth green, I walked over to the ball washer, and all of a sudden I saw that I had a strange ball in my hand. I'd mistaken it for my ball in the rough back there on the fifth hole.

I said to the other girls in my foursome, "Well, that's it. I've been playing the wrong ball. I've disqualified myself."

Nobody else ever would have known the difference if I'd kept quiet about it. But I'd have known the difference. I wouldn't have felt right in my own mind. You have to play by the rules of golf, just as you have to live by the rules of life. There's no other way.

Bob Mathias first won the Olympic decathlon
at the age of 17, a boy winning in a man's
world. In 1952 he repeated the feat. Although
the cold war was raging, Mathias had the
wisdom to see beyond the pale of politics to
the larger truths of brotherhood and humanity.
He saw his Russian competitors as...

MEN...NOT NATIONS

If they weren't wearing red jerseys I couldn't have told them from the athletes of other countries. They have the same desires and emotions as our athletes, and they behave just as we do in victory and defeat.

They're good athletes, all right. They've already proved that. I feel that competing against other nations is a fine thing for them. They're finding out that we're not so bad after all, and we're learning the same thing about them.

They've been fair and square in all the events I've seen them in, and they seem to enjoy the competition as genuinely as we do.

The idea of the Olympic Games is to foster international good will and sportsmanship. That has been accomplished here. After all, the Games are contests between individuals and not nations. So it's up to us competitors to form friendships.

Some men have a calling to be more than the best in their profession. Bill Russell, former captain and coach of the champion Boston Celtics, was perhaps the best basketball player of his time. But he knows the really BIG game is played off the hardwood, out in the real world. Bill Russell stands 6'10". In every sense of the phrase, Bill Russell is...

A BIG MAN

I am, in the final sense, just a man. I am neither all right nor all wrong. I was born in this nation, in this century. I was born to be a member of the nation, a member of the century, a member of the world.

A man, nothing more.

Neither right nor wrong.

Maybe I've soured on life, or maybe I'm a cynic, but I wasn't born that way. Maybe, I am an idealist — a frustrated idealist — but I wasn't born that way either. Things that I have experienced have made me what I am.

All I have finally asked is for everybody to succeed or fail on their own merits. I have tried to have a difference in values as values are computed in our modern society. I have worked hard for money. But I have not worshiped it.

I have never worked to be well-liked or well-loved, but only to be respected. I have fought a problem the only way I know how. Maybe it was right or wrong in the approach, but a man can only ultimately be counted if he thinks he is doing right. Then, at least, he is a man....

I have my own ideas for the future.

I have my own hopes and my own dreams.

I believe that I can contribute something far more important than mere basketball.

I said before three emotions have always been very real to me — fear, prejudice and bitterness.

It is the reactions to these emotions that make a man.

In the end, I live with the hopes that when I die, it will be inscribed for me:

Bill Russell.

He was a man.

DEFEAT

...if I lose, I'll walk away and never feel bad...Because I did all I could, there was nothing more to do.

JOE FRAZIER
as world heavyweight champion

A man who rode to many victories in the Kentucky Derby, a scrapper who wormed his way up from the poverty of the Pennsylvania coal fields to the top of his profession, jockey Bill Hartack says...

ONLY RESULTS COUNT!

There's only one thing that counts. Words don't mean anything. They can misquote me all they want or write something bad about me, but the only thing that counts is the chart of last Saturday's race. It says Venetian Way, number one. It don't say nothing else. And nobody can change it. Everything else, they can have. The only thing I'm accountable for in this business is the race I ride. I have to stand up for the owner of the horse, the trainer and the people who bet on him. And I have to see another jock doesn't get hurt because of me. I don't have to worry about anything else....

I do my job. I do what I think best. If I make a mistake, that's that. But the only place a mistake shows is the official chart of a race. If I don't win, that's a mistake. Nothing else counts. Not you or anybody else. Only that result.

Set in Primer, a crisp, modern
typeface created by Rudolph Ruzicka.
Printed on Hallmark Crown Royale Book paper.
Designed by Joel Ravitch.